To: Jerry E

From~

Merry Christmas!

The Heart & Home of Christmas

Peace to all who enter here

Karla Dornacher

COUNTRYMAN®

✩ ✩ ✩

Dear Friend,

There are so many things to love about Christmas...carols that sing of Jesus' birth and joy to the world, the scents of the season that fill the air and tempt our tummies, the radiant beams of light from rooftops to treetops, and the sight of our homes and hearths decorated to usher in this most joyous season of the year. It is a season marked by giving and sharing and caring. Christmas truly is the most beautiful holiday of them all...Beautiful to behold with the eye and with the heart!

I pray that through the pages of this little book you will be drawn close to Jesus, the One whose birthday we celebrate. It is my hope that through the sights and symbolism of the season you will be smitten with His glory and will invite Him to fill your heart and home with His incredible love today, throughout the holiday season, and into the coming new year.

Let us worship and adore Him together!

With love and joy...
Karla

Blessed be the Name of the Lord

Light of the World   Gift of God   The Door

The Living Word   God with Us   King of Kings

Prince of Peace   Bread of Life   Lamb of God

Salvation has come to this home today

Luke 19:9 NLT

Christmas is a special time of year,
a season set apart from all others to celebrate a miracle.
And what an incredible miracle it was!
God came into this world to bring us the gift of salvation.
In fact, He was the Gift!

Salvation was born that Christmas Day so long ago.
He wasn't delivered to a mansion or a motel.
His crib was not found in a townhouse or a ranch house.
No fancy wrapping or ribbon either.
Sent by the hand of God,
Salvation entered this world in a borrowed stable,
always looking...ever seeking...for a home to call His own.

Since the day He was born, Jesus has been knocking on doors
throughout the generations, among every culture and people.
He longs to find a home—a dwelling place—
in the hearts of people who will simply believe.

Yes, Christmas is a time to celebrate ... to rejoice ...
not only in the miracle of Christ's birth,
but with even deeper joy
we celebrate the miracle of His being born into our lives,
making His home in our hearts.

The Door

I have set before you an open Door
and invite you to enter in
to a season of life filled with love
and goodwill toward all men.

I stand at the Door to greet you
My arms are open wide
Come, enter in just as you are
and stay close by my side

I will lead you out of darkness
and into eternal light
through the Door of grace and glory
born that Christmas night.

For I am the Door to the Kingdom.
My Name is Immanuel.
Rejoice, My child, your Savior lives
and within your heart I dwell.

Peace to all who enter here

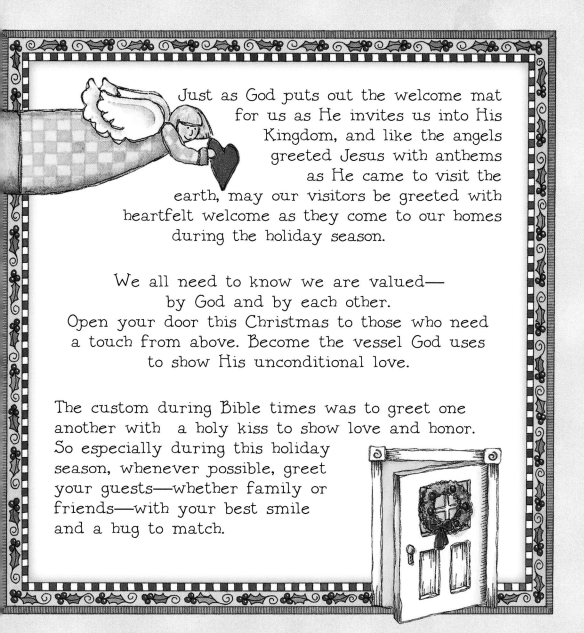

Just as God puts out the welcome mat
for us as He invites us into His
Kingdom, and like the angels
greeted Jesus with anthems
as He came to visit the
earth, may our visitors be greeted with
heartfelt welcome as they come to our homes
during the holiday season.

We all need to know we are valued—
by God and by each other.
Open your door this Christmas to those who need
a touch from above. Become the vessel God uses
to show His unconditional love.

The custom during Bible times was to greet one
another with a holy kiss to show love and honor.
So especially during this holiday
season, whenever possible, greet
your guests—whether family or
friends—with your best smile
and a hug to match.

What Child is this, Who, laid to rest,
On Mary's lap is sleeping?
Whom angels greet with anthems sweet,
While shepherds watch are keeping?

This, this is Christ the King,
Whom shepherds guard and angels sing:
Haste, haste to bring Him laud,
The Babe, the Son of Mary!

Welcome the season...
in His Name

The Door

Let your own personal taste,
creativity, and budget guide you
as you dress up your doorway to
bless the Lord and greet your guests.

Decorate a simple wreath to welcome
your guests with the Names of Jesus
written on bright colored ornaments.

Hang a banner that declares
the true Reason for the season.

Keep a basket of inexpensive
candies or gifts beside your door
with a tag that says, "In remembrance
of the greatest Gift ever given."
Give them to guests as they leave.

Jesus is
the reason!

Splendor
and majesty
are before
Him;
Strength
and joy
in His
dwelling
place.

1 Chronicles 16:27
NIV

When Jesus was born, God decorated the skies with heavenly fireworks to introduce the Light of the world. He scheduled the angelic choir to announce the Lamb of God to the lowly shepherds, and He sent a star to lead the kings from the East to worship the King of all kings.

Considering God decorated the heavens—His own dwelling place—it seems no less fitting for us to dress up our homes with strings of lights, carols that worship His Name, and symbols and seasonal reminders to help us celebrate the birth of His Son.

Some say that the Christmas tree, the candles, and other such trimmings belong to the pagan past; I believe all things belong to God—and we have simply reclaimed them for His glory!

This year, as you decorate your home, delight in the symbolism of the season and thank the Lord for the reminders they are... of Who He is and of why He came.

*"I am like a tree that is always green,
giving my fruit to you all through the year."*
Hosea 14:8 TLT

After almost getting our car stuck in the mud and sloshing for hours in slimy sludge, we returned home empty~handed. I had my version of the perfect tree in mind, but four tree lots later, we gave up and I gave in.
Our traditional trek to cut our own tree became but a fond memory.

I still cringe at the word "artificial," but I'm getting used to it. I remind myself that it's not the kind of tree one has—real or fake, stately or scraggly, noble or pine—but the symbolism that points the heart heavenward.

The evergreen tree was first used in celebration of a false god by people who did not know Jesus, the Creator of this symbol of everlasting life. As those who know Him and love Him, we have redeemed its value and given it a place of honor in our celebration of the only True God, who created all things for His glory.

As you set up your tree, remember that Jesus is like an evergreen . . . eternal and everlasting. With Him there is no beginning or end. And one day we will live in eternity with Him!

Heavenly Father, thank You that not only is Jesus like a tree, but that He died on a tree to save us from our sins, so that through faith in Him we could have eternal and everlasting life.

It's beginning to look
a lot like Christmas~
the tree is
standing tall~
and each ornament
that you place
reminds you of
God's grace
and His love
for one and all.

Merry Christmas

Joy to the world

21

Come to an Ornament Party!

You're invited to come and join us, please,
as we exchange ornaments to hang on our trees.
It's an opportunity to see old friends and new,
to visit, to laugh, and make memories, too!
So choose an ornament that reflects who you are...
do you sew, do you garden, do you collect stars?
As we trade ornaments,
we'll get to know one another
and celebrate the gift
of loving each other.

DATE: _____ TIME: _____

ADDRESS: _____

_____

_____

_____

RSVP: _____

_____

_____

_____

YOU HAVE MY BLESSING TO COPY THIS PAGE. HAVE A PARTY!

Merry Christmas

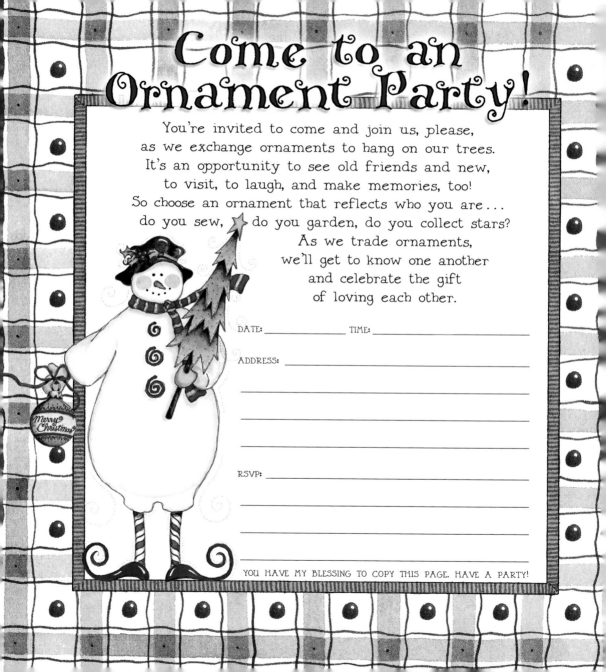

Deck the halls...
in His Name

A holiday ornament exchange
is a wonderful way to pass on the gift
of God's love to others.

Warm up someone else's life by asking each guest
to bring a blanket or winter coat along with their
ornament to the party. Give your donations to a
local church closet, charity or homeless shelter to
bring holiday hope and a touch of Christmas
comfort to those in need.

Do you remember how sparsely decorated your
first Christmas tree was? If you know
a single woman who has just moved
into her first apartment or a
newlywed couple celebrating
their first Christmas together,
invite your guests to bring
an extra ornament to create
a collection that will decorate
someone else's heart and home
with the Reason for the season.

Silent Night
Holy Night

The stars
in the sky
looked
down where
He lay

"Come to me, all you who are weary and burdened, and I will give you rest."

Matthew 11:28 NIV

Christmas is the most loving, giving, joyful holiday of the year. And yet it can be the most burdensome season as well. So much to do and so little time to do it! The voices of expectation vie for our attention. Perfect presents cry out to be purchased. The house and hearth long to be dressed. Parties and programs invite us to attend. And the list goes on and on and on! The sad truth is that we can become weary of Christmas just thinking about it!

But, shhhh!
If you can hush the holiday clatter for just a moment you will hear another Christmas voice, a quiet calling from the Baby in the manger. "Come to Me," He bids. Not demanding, but with a gentle spirit, He invites you to lay aside the heavy burden of the season and "find rest for your soul." He yearns for you to trade your unrealistic expectations for a season of heartfelt celebration!

To help you stay focused on the Heart of the season, choose a quiet place to set a nativity scene (even if it is in the bathroom) and find some quiet moments every day this month to hold the Baby Jesus in your hands and know that He holds you in His.

Lord Jesus, forgive me for listening to all the other voices before I've listened to Yours. I want this Christmas to be different . . . I want it to be all about You! Help me to lay aside all my expectations, to set aside time to be with You, and to know You're with me.

Prince of Peace

Have you ever yearned for a knight in shining armor
to come and rescue you from the struggles and chaos of your
life ... especially during the Christmas season?
Yearn no longer!
The One whose birthday you celebrate is the Prince of Peace,
and He has come to rescue you from fear and anxiety—
to give you a peace that will make your heart sing.

If you long for less stress and more peace of God,
I suggest you decorate the season with prayer!

Whether it's planning for your holiday activities or dealing with
the unexpected, hanging ornaments or standing in a checkout lane,
Jesus—the Prince of Peace—wants to give order to your chaos,
meaning to your activities, and calm to your heart.

Begin today to thank Him for what you love about Christmas.
(You'll think of more things in the days to come!)
Confide in Him about the things you don't like about the season.
(He knows your heart already.)
Ask Him for the wisdom to change what you are able
and the grace to transform
holiday hassles into holy~day opportunities!

Dear Jesus, thank You for being my Prince of Peace. Help me to
decorate my life with the ornaments of prayer and praise,
so that I may be like a tree of life to those around me.

Prince of Peace

There hangs a dove upon my tree
clothed in purest white,
a reminder of God's precious love
born that Christmas night.

The dove was once an offering,
part of God's great plan
to bring purity and peace between
God and sinful man.

But now there is an offering
for all mankind to see—
the pure and spotless sacrifice
of Christ upon the tree.

And the Prince of Peace lives again,
within your heart to dwell,
to give you life and bring you peace—
Jesus, Immanuel.

Because He sits upon His throne
the Holy Spirit has come
in the form of a dove from above
to make our hearts His home.

So let the Spirit remind you
as you see this Christmas dove
of the peace of God that's yours to have,
this sign of God's great love!

Be anxious for nothing,
but in everything by prayer
and supplication, with thanksgiving, let your
request be made known
to God, and the peace of God,
which surpasses all understanding,
will guard your hearts and mind
through Christ Jesus.

PHILIPPIANS 4:6, 7 NKJV

God rest ye merry, gentlemen,
Let nothing you dismay.
For Jesus Christ, our Savior,
Was born upon this day
To save us all from Satan's pow'r
When we were gone astray.

O tidings of comfort and joy,
Comfort and joy,
O tidings of comfort and joy.

Decorate the season...
in His Name

Decorate this holiday
season with ornaments
of praise and thanksgiving!
Use the symbols of the season
as reminders to stir your
faith in the Christ of Christmas, and watch how
your gratitude will guard your heart.

Slow down and savor a moment as you send out
and receive Christmas cards this year.
Let them spur you to pray for those special
people in your life. Pray that they, too, would
look to the Prince of Peace this Christmas season
and find rest for their souls.

Blessed is
she who has
believed...

Luke 1:45

Can you even begin to imagine what it must have been like for Mary?
Seeing an angel up close and personal is one thing,
but to have that angel tell you you're going to have a baby
when you've never been with a man could easily be unsettling.
A virgin having a baby . . . and not just your average baby either.
The angel told Mary she would be pregnant with a miracle.
She would give birth to the Son of God!
The question is still asked among us today . . . is this possible?

I love Mary's heart . . . and her example.
Though she did not understand it . . . she accepted it.
Though her future was unsure . . . she chose to believe.
The angel reminded her that with God nothing is impossible,
thus encouraging her faith, and Mary responded,
"Behold, the maidservant of the Lord!
Let it be to me according to your word" (LUKE 1:38 NKJV).
And so, the virgin gave birth to a Son,
and they called His name Immanuel, which means "God with us."

Maybe you need a Christmas miracle.
To be pregnant with the hope of the impossible.
To have relationships restored. Dreams renewed.
Hurts healed. Hearts comforted. To see God with you in a real way.

Mary pondered these things in her heart . . . will you?
God is truly with you and wants to birth a miracle in your life.
Remember . . . blessed is she who has believed!

God with Us

Away in a manger,
no crib for a bed,
the little Lord Jesus
laid down His sweet head;
the stars in the sky
looked down where He lay,
the little Lord Jesus
asleep on the hay.

Be near me, Lord Jesus,
I ask Thee to stay
close by me forever,
and love me, I pray;
bless all the dear children
in Thy tender care,
and fit us for heaven
to live with
Thee there.

Celebrate the season...

in His Name

Son of God

God is with you and it's His birthday! So bake a cake, light the candles, and invite your friends, family, and the kids from the neighborhood to celebrate His birth. After you sing "Happy Birthday" to Jesus, you might want to move the party outside and go caroling throughout your neighborhood.

Another good way to celebrate the birth of any baby is to host a baby shower. This Christmas consider having a baby shower in His Name and donating the gifts to a local pregnancy center.

O holy night,
when God became man,
knowing how dark it would be.
But He loved us so much
He gave up His life to give us eternity.

Mary held Him close
from the moment He was born,
knowing He was sent from above.
But her mother's heart
also ached for Him
who was born to die for love.

As pure as the snow
He entered this world—
no sin in a sin~filled earth.
But He took our sins,
washed us white as snow.
O come, celebrate His birth!

Pure as snow from heaven above

born a babe, God's gift of love

Now unto the
King eternal,
immortal, invisible,
the only wise God,
be honor and glory
forever and ever.
Amen.

1 TIMOTHY 1:17 KJV

40

Jesus was not born to become a King . . . He already was one.
It is almost unfathomable to consider that His royal reign
began long before He entered this world.

Even more amazing is that He was willing to lay aside His
heavenly robes and put on the humble garment
of human flesh for us—for you and me.
The King walked among us
so we could see Him and touch Him.
So we could know Him and love Him.
So we could believe in Him and allow Him
to rule and to reign over our hearts!

Jesus is King and He was born in a manger so we could know
that His Kingdom is not about what we have
or what we don't have.
It's not about wearing royal robes or buying expensive gifts.
God's Kingdom is about putting on the garments of love and
humility and giving ourselves to care for others.
That's what Jesus did.
And He became like us, so we could become like Him.
That's what Christmas is all about.

Will you invite Him to reign
over your heart and your home this holiday season?

Rejoice, o daughter of the King.
Lift up your heart to Him and sing!

Jesus

King of Kings

Worship the season...
in His Name

King of Kings

We worship the King not only with songs but with our lives. When we serve others, we are serving the Lord.

Reach out beyond your own home and family this year. Adopt a family going through a difficult time, and show them the generous love of God. Offer to help a single mom who doesn't have a way to bring home a tree.

Perhaps someone you know is suffering from a seasonal flu or a serious illness and could use the gift of helping hands. Gather your family and serve at a homeless shelter or charity organization.

Love lavishly this season!

Hark!
the herald angels sing,
"Glory to the newborn King!
Peace on earth, and mercy mild,
God and sinners reconciled."
Joyful, all ye nations rise,
Join the triumph of the skies;
With th' angelic host proclaim,
"Christ is born in Bethlehem."

Mild He lays His glory by,
Born that man
no more may die;
Born to raise the sons of earth,
Born to give them second birth.

Hark the herald angels sing

Glory to the newborn King

When I was a child, we piled into the car every Christmas Eve to drive through the streets of the city and oooooh and aaaaah over the dazzling displays of Christmas lights. The illumination of this special night announced the coming of Christmas, and with great anticipation and no arguments, we made haste up the stairs and into bed as soon as we arrived home.

Even now as an adult, a sense of awe and wonder rises in my heart to see the world all lit up. No matter how old or young we are . . . we long for the light. God made us that way. In our darkest hours and our deepest sorrows, in our daily struggles, and especially during the holiday season, we long for the light.

The Bible tells us that Jesus is the Light we have longed for. He wants to restore a sense of childlike awe and wonder into your life this Christmas. He was born to shine His love and His life into your heart and your home.

Let the Light of Christ shine brightly in and through you this Christmas. Keep your eyes on Jesus, and He will light the way for you to have a wonderful and worship~filled holiday season.

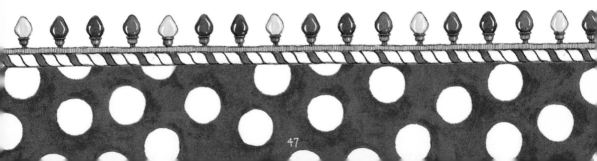

Light of the World

Arise, shine;
For your light has come!
And the glory of the LORD
is risen upon you.

Isaiah 60:1 NKJV

Jesus said to the people
"I am the Light
of the world."

John 8:12 NLT

We have seen His glory,
the glory of the only Son
of the Father.

John 1:14 NLT

The One who is the True Light,
who gives light to everyone,
was going to come into the world.

JOHN 1:9 NLT

O star of wonder, star of light,
Star with royal beauty bright,
Westward leading still proceeding,
Guide us to Thy perfect light.

It was the glory of the Lord that shone around the shepherds
as the angels guided them to the Light of the world.

It was a blazing celestial star that led the Magi to find the Light
that had been born into the world in Bethlehem.

And it is you and I who have now been entrusted with the Light.
God wants you to let your light shine so brightly
that others may see your good works and glorify God...
not your good works of buying and cooking and wrapping...
but your good works of loving and giving and caring.
To God, you are like a star with royal beauty bright,
guiding others to the perfect Light of Christ.

Light up the season...

in His Name

Light of the World

If you are in a Bible study group or home fellowship, give each person a single white candle to represent the Light of Christ. Attach a tag with a red ribbon and a verse about Jesus being the Light, or include a prayer asking God to let His Light shine brightly in their lives during this holiday.

Another bright and inexpensive way to let your light shine to those visiting your home is to line your walkway with luminaries.
Simply use grocery store lunchbags, white or brown paper, and cut a single star from each side. Place a votive candle on top of a two~inch layer of sand or kitty litter in the bottom of each bag, and then light the candle.

Candy and cookies and eggnog...oh my! Christmas is, without a doubt, the most delicious season of the year! And I love every bite of it!

The traditional tastes of the holiday are everywhere we go— from family dinners to office parties, from gifts of home~baked cookies to candy canes being offered as we shop.

Food is very much a part of our Christmas celebration. Sharing a meal with family or friends and giving away homemade goodies are festive and tasty ways to both feed the body and nurture the soul.

As gratifying as a full tummy and time spent with those you love may be, there is a hunger in your heart that longs to be fed, too...a hunger for the good things of the Lord.

God wants you to taste and see that He is good, to feed your heart just as you feed your body.

Look for ways to fill your home with God's Word and to feed the hearts of your family and friends this holiday season. Read the Christmas story aloud with your family. Write encouraging Scriptures in your holiday cards. Share the symbolism of the season in creative ways.

Jesus told us that He is the Bread of Life because only He can satisfy this hunger of your heart. May the sweetness of His love bring the most delightful flavor to your holiday season this year!

He satisfies the thirsty and fills the hungry with good things.

Psalm 107:9

Bread of Life

There is a story in the Bible about two women—
two ordinary women—just like you and me.
A story that remind me of today's Christmas.

When Martha heard that Jesus was in town, she invited Him
and all His friends to dinner. She was so excited to celebrate
His coming—to honor and bless Him.
She set about planning the perfect meal, decorating the house,
hanging ornaments on the tree, making and
wrapping gifts for everyone. But before long she became so
distracted with all of her busyness that she was no longer
thinking about the Guest of honor. She had lost her focus.
Jesus was no longer the reason for her work
or her celebration.

Martha became frustrated and asked Jesus to speak to her
sister, Mary, because instead of joining her in her
busyness, Mary had chosen to sit at Jesus' feet.

Jesus replied, "Martha, Martha . . . you worry about so much
unnecessary stuff. Mary has chosen to celebrate My coming by
spending time with Me, and she has chosen the better way."

Maybe if Martha had prepared a simple meal . . . a meal that
honored His humble birth . . . she, too, might have had time to
enjoy the celebration. Be encouraged to simplify your season.

What will you choose this day?
I pray for you the better way.

Christmas Soup in a Jar Recipe

Bean Soup Mix

black beans   red beans   kidney beans
navy beans   great northern beans   baby lima beans
large lima beans   pinto beans   green split peas
yellow split peas   black~eyed peas
green lentils   brown lentils

   Choose and combine equal amounts of beans and pour 2 cups of mix into each jar (16 oz.). Or layer a little of each bean for a prettier look.

Holiday Bean Soup

To: **From:**

Bean Soup Mix from jar   6 cups water
1 smoked ham hock   1/4 cup fresh parsley
  2 cans stewed tomatoes   1 Tbsp red wine vinegar
  1 med. onion, chopped   2 tsp salt
    1 tsp chili powder   1 tsp cumin seed

   Cover beans with water and soak overnight. Drain beans and place in a stockpot. Add remaining ingredients and bring to a boil over med~high heat. Cover and simmer one hour or until beans are tender. Makes 11 cups.

Nourish the season...
in His Name

Bread of Life

Offer a taste of God's grace
and goodness to a hungry
world this Christmas
by giving the gift of food
or volunteering to help serve
meals at a homeless shelter.

Designate a generous portion of your gift~giving
budget to donate to an organization such as Feed
the Children or Samaritan's Purse. You can look
these up on the Internet for more information.

Simplify your labor this season by simplifying
your menus. Let soup and bread be a frequent
meal to remind you and your family and even
your guests of the humble beginnings of
the Bread of Life.

We three kings of Orient are bearing gifts, we traverse afar,
field and fountain, moor and mountain, following yonder star.

For most of us, this familiar carol inspires images of camels
and a cast of royal characters on a journey
to give gifts to the One who was born the King of the Jews.
Kings greeting the King of all kings.
Gifts given to the Greatest Gift of all gifts.

God's gift to you this Christmas is His love—
a gift from God's own heart to yours.
He wrapped His love in His Son, Jesus, and sent Him to you.
Can you see your name on the tag below?
If it's not there, write it in ... God already has.

He was thinking of you when He came.
He was thinking of you when He died.
He's thinking of you right now.

God adores you! Will you worship and adore Him?

Will you join with other believers this Christmas ...
love them with the love God's given to you ...
and praise Him for His incredible Gift?

Jesus

Gift of God

God has a special Gift for you,
but it's not beneath the tree.
He wrapped it up in swaddling cloths
tied with humility.

But don't let the wrappings fool you,
its value exceeds measure,
for of greater worth than precious gold
is this priceless treasure.

Hold out your hands, open up your heart,
and lift your eyes to see,
for this Gift of God is Jesus Christ
hung upon the tree.

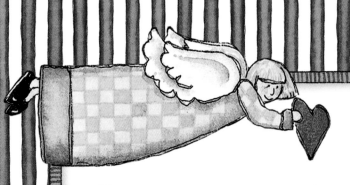

For God so loved the world
that He gave His only Son,
so that everyone
who believes in Him
will not perish
but have eternal life.

JOHN 3:16 NLT

Give this season...
in His Name

To give in the Name of Jesus means giving from the heart, not just buying something because it's expected.

This year pray for each person on your shopping list. Ask God to give you wisdom as you make or buy your gifts this year.

You may be surprised at how creative God can be. You may also be encouraged, because He already knows your budget and would never have you spend more than you can afford.

All this took place to fulfill what the Lord had said through the prophet: "The virgin will be with child and will give birth to a son..." Matthew 1:22,23 NIV

The Bible tells us that God had a plan from the beginning of time to send His Son to save us from our sins. With His celestial calendar in hand, He laid out the events of history and then gave hints through prophecy as to when this grand event would occur. He chose the place, the people, the date and time, even the choir delegated to sing. All this took place to fulfill what the Lord had planned... the greatest birthday in history. A celebration that would divide time and alter calendars. A celebration that is still the talk of all mankind!

If God took the time to plan out the celebration of the season, wouldn't it be wise for us to do the same?

As early as possible, get out your earthly calendar and pray over it. Enter in the family, friend, work, or school events that are most important. Remember to include choir practice or play rehearsals! Most importantly, mark off time to stay home and give your family a time of rest and refocus by reading the Christmas story together and rejoicing in the Living Word.

His
name is
called
The
Word of God

Revelation 19:13

In the beginning was the Word. The Word was with God, and the Word was God. He was with God in the beginning.

All things were made by Him, and nothing was made without Him. In Him there was life, and that life was the light of all people. The

was coming into this world!

The Word was in the world, and the world was made by Him, but the world did not know Him. He came to the world which was His own, but His own people did not accept Him. But to all who did

accept Him and believe in Him, He gave the right to become children of God. They did not become His children in any human way—by two parents. They were born of God.

Living Word

In the beginning was the Word,
and the Word was with God,
and the Word was God.
He was in the beginning with God.
All things were made through Him,
and without Him
nothing was made that was made.

And the Word became flesh
and dwelt among us,
and we beheld His glory,
the glory as of
the only begotten of the Father,
full of grace and truth.

JOHN 1:1~3, 14 NKJV

Dear Jesus,

I pray this Christmas season
that Your Word would dwell in me richly,
that the Bible would not just be words on a page,
but that they would come alive
and speak to my heart.

I long to draw close to You,
to know You in a deeper way
throughout this season
and into the coming New Year.
I want to know You, Jesus,
not just as the Baby in the manger,
but as my Redeemer and Savior,
the One who was born to rescue me
from sin and death
and give me eternal life.

Make Your home in my heart, Lord.

In Your precious Name,
Amen

Herald the season...

in His Name

The Bible is the written Word of God, an expression of His love. Jesus was the living expression of God's love to us. May your words speak love and value everywhere you go!

A great way to share the Living Word is to donate money to organizations that translate and give Bibles to those who have never heard the Good News.

Another way to herald the Good News of the season is to offer to read and address greeting cards for the elderly.

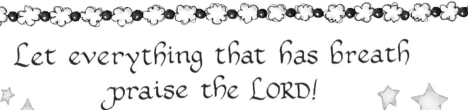

Let everything that has breath praise the LORD!

Psalm 150:6 NKJV

There was a man in the Bible,
who when the world around him seemed to be
chaotic and meaningless, made a decision.
He said, "As for me and my house, we will serve the LORD"
(Joshua 24:15 NKJV). You can make this choice, too.
Choose this year to make your home a place where Jesus is honored.
Do your best to dwell on what is right with Christmas
rather than focusing on what is wrong with it.

Use the signs and symbols of the season
to remind you of the Names of Jesus and who He is to you.
Decide to make this Christmas more about Him
and less about stuff by giving away the best gift
that was ever given to you—
the unconditional, unmerited, everlasting love of God!

Dedicate this season to worship the Lord
by being His heart, His hands,
and His voice to those around you,
and let heaven and nature sing!

Lamb of God

Sacrifice the season...
in His Name

Lamb of God

Give yourself away generously!
The sacrifice of your time, talent,
or money may open the door for
others to see the salvation of
the Lord in their lives.
Consider giving, not just out of
your abundance, but actually giving
up something in order to help someone
who needs a touch of God's love.

Maybe this is the year to help
your children understand
that Christmas is not
just about giving to our
own families and friends—
but giving to those who have
nothing to give in return.

You are God's workmanship

EPHESIANS 2:10

My granddaughters love to play in the snow!
They fall backwards into the downy softness
and wave their little arms to create beautiful
snow angels, and then they giggle at their creations.
Lying in the cold snow is one thing, but there's
just something about rolling a snowperson with
one's hands that means Grandma has to join in.
Together this jolly~looking creature becomes our
workmanship, created to bring smiles and joy
to all who pass by.

As I create this wonderful fellow I am
reminded of God's most prized creation—us!

We are God's handiwork.

God formed us in our mothers' wombs
and set us apart for Himself
before we were even born.
He had a plan all along.
A plan to be born in a manger, live among us,
and die on the cross so our sins could be
forgiven and we could be washed
white as the new~fallen snow.

*Celebrating Christ's birthday
is celebrating the life
He died to give us.*

And being found in appearance
as a man, He humbled Himself and
became obedient to the point of death,
even the death of the cross.
Therefore God also has highly exalted
Him and given Him the name which
is above every name, that at the name
of Jesus every knee should bow,
of those in heaven and those on earth,
and of those under the earth, and that every
tongue should confess that Jesus Christ is
Lord, to the glory of the Father.

PHILIPPIANS 2:8~11 NKJV

 Dear Friend,

Christmas truly is the most beautiful season of the year
and I appreciate being able to share some of its beauty
with you in my own unique way.
I hope you have been encouraged
to keep your eyes on Jesus, the true Reason for the season,
and find comfort, hope, and joy in His Name.

Jesus came to seek and save the lost.
That's what Christmas is really all about.
The Bible tells us that there is no other name in all of heaven
that a person can call upon to be saved.
If you have never experienced the true joy of Christmas—
the joy that abides in the heart long after the tree comes down
and all the stockings are put away—Jesus is calling your name!
All you have to do is open the door to your heart
and invite Him in.

Thank God for the precious Gift of His Son.
Ask the perfect Lamb of God to forgive your sins
and wash you white as snow.
Invite Him to reign in your life as the King of kings,
and begin today to experience the peace that only
the Prince of Peace can give.
Take time to eat from the Bread of Life,
and you will come to know Him as the Living Word!
God is with us . . . God is with you!

Praying you have the lightest, brightest Christmas ever!

In His love and for His glory! Karla

For more information
on my other books and gift products
or to share your thoughts or comments,
please write, email,
or check out my website . . .
I'd love to hear from you!

Karla Dornacher
P.O. Box 185 ♥ Battle Ground, WA 98604
Karla@KarlaDornacher.com
www.KarlaDornacher.com